China Trace

CHINA

TRACE

by
Charles Wright

WESLEYAN UNIVERSITY PRESS

Middletown, Connecticut 06457

Acknowledgment is gratefully made to the following pe-
riodicals, in the pages of which all the poems in this
book were first published: *The American Poetry Review,
The American Review, Antaeus, The Atlantic Monthly,
Chiaroscuro, The Chicago Review, Choice, Cold Spring
Journal, Field, Greenhouse Review, Grove, The Iowa Re-
view, Marilyn, Occident, The Ohio Review, Pocket Pal,
The Pomegranate Press Broadsides, Red Weather, Three
Rivers Poetry Journal, The University of Connecticut
Broadside Series, The Vanderbilt Poetry Review* and *The
New Yorker* ("Childhood," "Sentences," "Edvard
Munch," "Remembering San Zeno," "Depression Before
the Solstice," "Stone Canyon Nocturne," "Noon" and
"Clear Night").

Section 1 was published as a chapbook in a limited edi-
tion under the title *Colophons* by The Windhover Press.

Grateful acknowledgment is also made to the John
Simon Guggenheim Foundation and to The National En-
dowment on the Arts for awards which significantly con-
tributed to the completion of this book.

Library of Congress Cataloging in Publication Data

Wright, Charles, 1935–
    China trace.

    (The Wesleyan poetry program ; v. 88)
    Poems.
    I. Title.
PS3573.R52C5   811'.5'4   77-74604
ISBN 0-8195-2088-8
ISBN 0-8195-1088-2 pbk.

Manufactured in the United States of America
First edition

For Luke Savin Herrick Wright

Mingliaotse: "I would like to house my spirit within my body, to nourish my virtue by mildness, and to travel in ether by becoming a void. But I cannot do it yet ... And so, being unable to find peace within myself, I made use of the external surroundings to calm my spirit, and being unable to find delight within my heart, I borrowed a landscape to please it. Therefore, strange were my travels."

— T'U LUNG [T'U CH'IHSHUI]
translated by Lin Yutang

Table of Contents

2.

1.

"On the day when I know all the emblems," Kublai Khan asked Marco, "shall I be able to possess my empire, at last?"

And the Venetian answered: "Sire, do not believe it. On that day you will be an emblem among emblems."

—ITALO CALVINO, *Invisible Cities*

Childhood

Shrunken and drained dry, turning transparent,
You've followed me like a dog
I see through at last, a window into Away-From-Here, a place
I'm headed for, my tongue loosened, tracks
Apparent, your beggar's-lice
Bleaching to crystal along my britches leg:

I'm going away now, goodbye.
Goodbye to the locust husk and the chairs;
Goodbye to the genuflections. Goodbye to the clothes
That circle beneath the earth, the names
Falling into the darkness, face
After face, like beads from a broken rosary . . .

Snow

If we, as we are, are dust, and dust, as it will, rises,
Then we will rise, and recongregate
In the wind, in the cloud, and be their issue,

Things in a fall in a world of fall, and slip
Through the spiked branches and snapped joints of the
        evergreens,
White ants, white ants and the little ribs.

Self-Portrait in 2035

The root becomes him, the road ruts
That are sift and grain in the powderlight
Recast him, sink bone in him,
Blanket and creep up, fine, fine:

Worm-waste and pillow tick; hair
Prickly and dust-dangled, his arms and black shoes
Unlinked and laceless, his face false
In the wood-rot, and past pause . . .

Darkness, erase these lines, forget these words.
Spider recite his one sin.

Morandi

I'm talking about stillness, the hush
Of a porcelain center bowl, a tear vase, a jug.

I'm talking about space, which is one-sided,
Unanswered, and left to dry.

I'm talking about paint, about shape, about the void
These objects sentry for, and rise from.

I'm talking about sin, red drop, white drop,
Its warp and curve, which is blue.

I'm talking about bottles, and ruin,
And what we flash at the darkness, and what for . . .

Dog

The fantailed dog of the end, the lights out,
Lopes in his sleep,
The moon's moan in the glassy fields.
Everything comes to him, stone
Pad prints extending like stars, tongue black
As a flag, saliva and thread, the needle's tooth,
Everything comes to him.

If I were a wind, which I am, if I
Were smoke, which I am, if I
Were the colorless leaves, the invisible grief,
Which I am, which I am,
He'd whistle me down, and down, but not yet.

Snapshot

Under the great lens of heaven, caught
In the flash and gun of the full moon,
Improbable target in the lunar click,

My own ghost, a lock-shot lanyard of blue flame,
Slips from the deadeyes in nothing's rig,
Raiment and sustenance, and hangs

Like a noose in the night wind. Or like a mouth,
O-fire in the scaffolding. You are wine
In a glass, it says, you are sack, you are silt.

Indian Summer

The plains drift on through the deep daylight.

I watch the snow bees sent mad by the sun.

The limbs of the hickory trees swing loose in the noontide,
Feathery, stretching their necks.

The wind blows through its own hair forever.

If something is due me still
—Firedogs, ashes, the soap of another life—
I give it back. And this hive

Of sheveled combs, my wax in its little box.

Wishes

I wish I were unencumbered, in Venice or South Bay.
I wish I were thrust down by enormous weights
Anywhere, anywhere.
I wish that the blood fly would crawl from its hiding place.

The sun slides up through the heat, and has no dreams.
The days drop, each nosed by the same dog.
In some other language,
I walk by this same river, these same vowels in my throat.

I wish I could say them now, returned
Through the dry thread of the leaf, the acorn's root.
It's somewhere I can't remember, but saw once.
It's late in the afternoon there.

Quotidiana

The moss retracts its skin from the laced grass.
This mist is a cold address,
This late light a street that others have moved from too.
The river stays shut, and writes my biography.

Midwinter, midwinter,
Your necktie of ice, your salt shoes,
Trees in a numb nudge, you
Come through the sand sieve, you bear me up.

At Zero

In the cold kitchen of heaven,
Daylight spoons out its cream-of-wheat.

Beside the sidewalk, the shrubs
Hunch down, deep in their bibs.

The wind harps its same song
Through the steel tines of the trees.

The river lies still, the jeweled drill in its teeth.

I am glint on its fingernails.
I am ground grains on its wheel.

Sentences

The ash fish has been away for a long time now,
The snow transparent; a white cane rakes back and forth
In the hush, no sweet sound from the leaves.

———

Whatever is dead stays dead: the lighted and cold
Blue blank pavilions of the sky,
The sand, the crystal's ring in the bushy ear—
Voices logy with sleep, their knapsacks
The color of nothing, full of the great spaces they still must
      cross.

———

The trees take care of their own salvation, and rocks
Swell with their business: and there, on the clean cloth
Of the river, a Host is floating without end.

———

Heaven, that stray dog, eats on the run and keeps moving.

Death

I take you as I take the moon rising,
Darkness, black moth the light burns up in.

Next

I am weary of daily things,
How the limbs of the sycamore
Dip to the snow surge and disaffect;
How the ice moans and the salt swells.
Where is that country I signed for, the one with the lamp,
The one with the penny in each shoe?

I want to lie down, I am so tired, and let
The crab grass seep through my heart,
Side by side with the inchworm and the fallen psalm,
Close to the river bank,
In autumn, the red leaves in the sky
Like lost flags, sidle and drift . . .

January

In some other life
I'll stand where I'm standing now, and will look down, and will
    see
My own face, and not know what I'm looking at.

These are the nights
When the oyster begins her pearl, when the spider slips
Through his wired rooms, and the barns cough, and the grass
    quails.

1975

Year of the Half-Hinged Mouth and the Hollow Bones,
Year of the Thorn,
Year of the Rope and the Dead Coal,
Year of the Hammering Mountain, Year of the Sponge . . .

I open the book of What I Can Never Know
To page 1, and start to read:
"The snow falls from the hills to the sea, from the cloud
To the cloud's body, water to water . . ."

At 40, the apricot
Seems raised to a higher power, the fire ant and the weed.
And I turn in the wind,
Not knowing what sign to make, or where I should kneel.

Nerval's Mirror

I'll never know what the clouds promised,
Or what the stars intended to say;
I'll never return the call of What's-To-Come.

I'm safe now, and well fed.
Don't look for me in the white night of the Arctic;
I'm floating here, my side iced to its side.

Edvard Munch

We live in houses of ample weight,
Their windows a skin-colored light, pale and unfixable.
Our yards are large and windraked, their trees bent to the
     storm.
People we don't know are all around us.

Or else there is no one, and all day
We stand on a bridge, or a cliff's edge, looking down.
Our mothers stare at our shoes.

Hands to our ears, our mouths open, we're pulled on
By the flash black, flash black flash of the lighthouse
We can't see on the rock coast,
Notes in a bottle, our lines the ink from the full moon.

Bygones

The rain has stopped falling asleep on its crystal stems

Equation

I open the phone book, and look for my adolescence.
How easy the past is—
Alphabetized, its picture taken,
It leans in the doorway, it fits in the back pocket.

The crime is invisible,
But it's there. Why else would I feel so guilty?
Why else would that one sorrow still walk through my sleep,
Looking away, dressed in its best suit?

I touch my palm. I touch it again and again.
I leave no fingerprint. I find no white scar.
It must have been something else,
Something enormous, something too big to see.

California Twilight

Late evening, July, and no one at home.
In the green lungs of the willow, fly-worms and lightning bugs
Blood-spot the whips and wings. Blue

Asters become electric against the hedge.
What was it I had in mind?
The last whirr of a skateboard dwindles down Oak Street hill.

Slowly a leaf unlocks itself from a branch.
Slowly the furred hands of the dead flutter up from their caves.
A little pinkish flame is snuffed in my mouth.

Anniversary

At dawn, in the great meadow, a solitude
As easy as white paint comes down from the mountains
To daydream, bending the grass.

I take my body, familiar bundle of sorrows, to be
Touched by its hem, and smoothed over . . .

There's only one secret in this life that's worth knowing,
And you found it.
                    I'll find it too.

12 Lines at Midnight

Sleep, in its burning garden, sets out the small plants.
Behind me an animal breaks down,
One ear to the moon's brass sigh.

The earth ticks open like a ripe fruit.
The mist, with sleeves of bone, slides out of the reeds,
Everything hushed, the emptiness everywhere.

The breath inside my breath is the breath of the dream.
I lick its charred heart, a piece of the same flaked sky
The badger drags to his hole.

The bread bleeds in the cupboard,
The mildew tightens. The clocks, with their tiny hands, reach
       out,
Inarticulate monitors of the wind.

Dino Campana

After the sad tunes on the dog's tooth,
The twistwort and starbane
—Blood lilies the heart breeds—,
Your mouth is the blue door I walk through,
The lamp lit, the table laid.

Scalp Mountain

This mountain is half-hinged, an unremembered transparency
We'll come to again, and pass through, a mirror
That gives back nothing, a throatless, untouchable pane of glass
     in the earth.

Invisible Landscape

This is the way it must have been in the first dusk:
Smokeclouds sculling into their slips in the Claw Mountains,
Bats jerked through the plumlight by strings of white sound;
The wind clicks through its turnstiles
Over the high country, the hush of a steady pulse . . .

I bring to this landscape a bare hand, these knuckles
Slick as a cake of soap,
The black snag of a tamarack,
The oddments and brown jewelry of early September evenings
In wet weather, a Colt-colored sky . . .

God is the sleight-of-hand in the fireweed, the lost
Moment that stopped to grieve and moved on . . .

2.

"On the day when I know all the emblems," Kublai Khan asked Marco, "shall I be able to possess my empire, at last?"

And the Venetian answered: "Sire, do not believe it. On that day you will be an emblem among emblems."

—ITALO CALVINO, *Invisible Cities*

Remembering San Zeno

After the end, they'll bring you
To someplace like this, columns of light propped through a
       west-facing door,
People standing about, echo of shoe-taps,
The gloom, like a grease-soaked rag, like a slipped skin
Left in a corner, puddled
In back of the votive stick stands, matter-of-factly—

Under the lisp and cold glow of the flames
Everything stares and moves closer, faces and blank hands,
October the 1st, 1975,
The banked candles the color of fresh bone,
Smoke rising from chimneys beyond the beyond,
Nightfires, your next address . . .

Born Again

Sunday night and a full moon,
October the 19th, moon-glyphs on the grass and leaves.
In the endless expanse of heaven,
3 stars break out through the cover-up, and hang free.
Behind the veneer of light and the scorched lungs
Are walks I will take.

Nothingness, tilt your cup.
I am the wafer just placed on your tongue,
The transubstantiation of bone and regret
To air and a photograph;
I am the diamond and bad heart,
Breath's waste, the slip-back and failure of What's Past.

Deep Water

The hardpan dust of the sky is criss-crossed and swept clean.
Who hears the mouth harp and its slow dance,
The chilled complaint of the sand?
Who cares if it counts my sins, and won't absolve?
Some things stay cold to exist: dry ice and the maimed child,
My hands, the nighttime and deep water. My hands.

Captain Dog

Another December, another year
Gone to the bleached Pacific, a little castle of snow
Falling across the sky
I wanted to linger in for awhile.

And so I lose touch, the walls, in their iced dismemberings,
Shrinking like aches, a slide and a by-your-leave.

The nights, with their starred palms, press down,
Black moths on the screen door,
Slow breaths to stop the body's bleeding, deep breaths.

I'm jump-cut and Captain Dog, staked
In the shadow of nothing's hand.
I bend like a finger joint, I gather, I burn.

— 1975

Depression Before the Solstice

4 days till the solstice, the moon
Like an onion thin in the afternoon sky, the few leaves
In the liquidambar arthritic and holding on.
The weightless, unclarified light from the setting sun
Lies like despair on the ginger root. Windows
Go up in flame. Now

The watchers and holy ones set out, divining
The seal, eclipses
Taped to their sleeves with black felt,
Their footprints filling with sparks
In the bitter loam behind them, ahead of them stobbed with
        sand,
And walk hard, and regret nothing.

Lips

My lips say what the lips in the west say
At evening, tomorrow flattening itself against the door,
Hammer that someday will send my friends to their knees,
That will pry my skin loose and start
My parents to preening inside their graves,
A yearn for the natural hug, the quick kiss overhead.

Stone Canyon Nocturne

Ancient of Days, old friend, no one believes you'll come back.
No one believes in his own life anymore.

The moon, like a dead heart, cold and unstartable, hangs by a
      thread
At the earth's edge,
Unfaithful at last, splotching the ferns and the pink shrubs.

In the other world, children undo the knots in their tally
      strings.
They sing songs, and their fingers blear.

And here, where the swan hums in his socket, where bloodroot
And belladonna insist on our comforting,
Where the fox in the canyon wall empties our hands, ecstatic
      for more,

Like a bead of clear oil the Healer revolves through the night
      wind,
Part eye, part tear, unwilling to recognize us.

Reply to Chi K'ang

There is no light for us at the end of the light.
No one redeems the grass our shadows lie on.

Each night, in its handful of sleep, the mimosa blooms.
Each night the future forgives.
Inside us, albino roots are starting to take hold.

Reunion

Already one day has detached itself from all the rest up ahead.
It has my photograph in its soft pocket.
It wants to carry my breath into the past in its bag of wind.

I write poems to untie myself, to do penance and disappear
Through the upper right-hand corner of things, to say grace.

"Where Moth and Rust Doth Corrupt"

No moon in the eastern sky, the Big Dipper
Spilling its nothingness from Baja to Prudhomme Bay,
Ashes strewn through my life like old clothes.
The outline of 10 crosses still dampens and stains my
        childhood,
Oppressive forehead, infinite hymn . . .

Lie back and regenerate,
                family of dust,
Invisible groom, father and son I step through.
Spread for the fly's fall,
Its body released and sucked clean and full of the air.
I whisper into a different ear.

I mimic the tongues of green flame in the grass.
I live in the one world, the moth and rust in my arms.

April

The plum tree breaks out in bees.
A gull is locked like a ghost in the blue attic of heaven.
The wind goes nattering on,
Gossipy, ill at ease, in the damp rooms it will air.
I count off the grace and stays
My life has come to, and know I want less—

Divested of everything,
A downfall of light in the pine woods, motes in the rush,
Gold leaf through the undergrowth, and come back
As another name, water
Pooled in the black leaves and holding me there, to be
Released as a glint, as a flash, as a spark . . .

Signature

> Don't wait for the snowfall from the dogwood tree.
> Live like a huge rock covered with moss,
> Rooted half under the earth
> > and anxious for no one.

Noon

I look up at the black bulge of the sky and its belt of stars,
And know I can answer to nothing in all that shine,
Desire being ash, and not remembered or brought back by the
      breath,
Scattered beneath the willow's fall, a figure of speech . . .

And know that what I have asked for cannot be granted, that
      what
Is waiting for me is laced in my 2 shoes,
Wind that will alter me, extension that one day will ease me on
In my slow rise through the dark toward the sweet wrists of
      the rose.

The dirt is a comforting, and the night drafts from the sucker
      vines.
The grass is a warm thing, and the hollyhocks, and the bright
      bursts from the weeds.
But best of all is the noon, and its tiny horns,
When shadows imprint, and start
                      their gradual exhalation of the past.

Guilt

Drop by drop it accrues, a faithless and fatherless medicine.

It is not written that Comfort is sure to arrive.
A teaspoon, a tablespoon,
This puddle becomes our dosage, and vast as the night's leaf.

Going Home

The ides of a hangdog month.
Dirt roads and small towns come forth
And fall from the pepper tree,
                              evening flashing their panes
And stray flakes through a thin drizzle of darkness,
Strikes in the dry fields of the past,
                              bonesparks
From the nailed feet that walk there.

I ask for a second breath,
Great Wind, where everything's necessary
And everything rises,
                              unburdened and borne away, where
The flash from the setting sun
Is more than a trick of light, where halflife
Is more than just a watery glow,
                              and everything's fire . . .

Cloud River

The unborn children are rowing out to the far edge of the sky,
Looking for warm beds to appear in. How lucky they are,
    dressed
In their lake-colored gowns, the oars in their oily locks
Taking them stroke by stroke to circumference and artery . . .

I'd like to be with them still, pulling my weight,
Blisters like small white hearts in the waxed palms of my
    hands.
I'd like to remember my old name, and keep the watch,
Waiting for something immense and unspeakable to uncover its
    face.

Reply to Lapo Gianni

Lapo, we're all slow orphans under the cruel sleep of heaven.
We're all either creased and sealed or somebody's cough.

Outside the window, twilight slips on its suede glove.
The river is fine balsam, fragrant and nicked by cold feathers.
Under the grass, the lights go on in their marled rooms.

Lapo, the dreams of the dog rose are nothing to you and me.

Thinking of Georg Trakl

August, the bones of summer, the chamber and last lunch
Before the fall. All day the creatures and small wings
Have hung back or held their tongues.
All day they have known what we will know when the time
        comes.

Sister of Mercies, a body is laid out, look,
Under the ghost light of the stars. 11:15. With different breaths,
Silently, up from the river, its wet-sheet of mist
Is drawn forth and arranged.

Lips part in the bleached willows.
Finger by finger, above Orion, God's blue hand unfolds.

Spider Crystal Ascension

The spider, juiced crystal and Milky Way, drifts on his web
    through the night sky
And looks down, waiting for us to ascend . . .

At dawn he is still there, invisible, short of breath, mending his
    net.

All morning we look for the white face to rise from the lake
    like a tiny star.
And when it does, we lie back in our watery hair and rock.

Moving On

Once it was lamb's fleece and the fall.
Once it was wedge of the eyelid and eyelid down to poison and
      sheer slumber,
The flesh made flesh and the word.

Now it's the crack in the porcelain stick,
And midnight splashed on the 1st rocks and gone,
The wafer of blood in its chalk robes,

The bright nail of the east I usher my body toward.

Clear Night

Clear night, thumb-top of a moon, a back-lit sky.
Moon-fingers lay down their same routine
On the side deck and the threshold, the white keys and the
     black keys.
Bird hush and bird song. A cassia flower falls.

I want to be bruised by God.
I want to be strung up in a strong light and singled out.
I want to be stretched, like music wrung from a dropped seed.
I want to be entered and picked clean.

And the wind says "What?" to me.
And the castor beans, with their little earrings of death, say
     "What?" to me.
And the stars start out on their cold slide through the dark.
And the gears notch and the engines wheel.

Autumn

November the 1st. Gold leaves
Whisper their sentences through the blue chains of the wind.
I open a saint-john's-bread.

Green apples, a stained quilt,
The black clock of the heavens reset in the future tense.
Salvation's a simple thing.

Sitting at Night on the Front Porch

I'm here, on the dark porch, restyled in my mother's chair.
10:45 and no moon.
Below the house, car lights
Swing down, on the canyon floor, to the sea.

In this they resemble us,
Dropping like match flames through the great void
Under our feet.
In this they resemble her, burning and disappearing.

Everyone's gone
And I'm here, sizing the dark, saving my mother's seat.

Saturday 6 a.m.

The month gone and the day coming up like a bad cold
Insistent behind the eyes, a fine sweat on the mustard stalks.
There's something I want to say,

But not here, stepped out and at large on the blurred hillside.
Over my shoulder, the great pane of the sunlight tilts toward
        the sea.
I don't move. I let the wind speak.

Him

His sorrow hangs like a heart in the star-flowered boundary
      tree.
It mirrors the endless wind.

He feeds on the lunar differences and flies up at the dawn.

When he lies down, the waters will lie down with him,
And all that walks and all that stands still, and sleep through
      the thunder.

It's for him that the willow bleeds.

Look for him high in the flat black of the northern Pacific sky,
Released in his suit of lights,
                             lifted and laid clear.

DEMCO